THE COOLEST JOBS ON THE PLANET

POLAR SCIENTIST

Emily Shuckburgh with Catherine Chambers

Raintree

Raintree is an imprint of Capstone Global Library Limited, a company incorporated in England and Wales having its registered office at 7 Pilgrim Street, London, EC4V 6LB – Registered company number: 6695582

To contact Raintree please phone 0845 6044371, fax + 44 (0) 1865 312263, or email myorders@raintreepublishers.co.uk. Customers from outside the UK please telephone +44 1865 312262.

Text © Capstone Global Library Limited 2015
First published in hardback in 2014
The moral rights of the proprietor have been asserted.

Edited by Andrew Farrow, Christine Peterson and Helen Cox Cannons
Designed by Cynthia Akiyoshi
Original illustrations © Capstone Global Library Limited 2014
Illustrated by HL Studios
Picture research by Mica Brancic and Tracy Cummins
Production by Helen McCreath
Originated by Capstone Global Library Limited
Printed and bound in China

ISBN 978 1 406 28011 1
18 17 16 15 14
10 9 8 7 6 5 4 3 2 1

British Library Cataloguing in Publication Data
A full catalogue record for this book is available from the British Library.

Acknowledgements
We would like to thank the following for permission to reproduce photographs: Alamy pp. 40-41 (© Rice Jackson); BAS pp. 4, 5, 26, 27, 28, 32, 33, 34, 35 (all Emily Shuckburgh), 11 (Agnieszka Fryckowska), 14 & 38 top (both Chris Gilbert), 19 (Bryn Jones), 20 (Teal Riley), 21 (Catherine Moore), 6, 22, 25, 37 & 38 bottom (all Pete Bucktrout), 23 (Sam Burrell), 36 (Roger Stilwell), 39 (Morag Hunter); Corbis Reuters/Alister Doyle p. 7; FLPA p. 15 (ImageBroker/Imagebroker); Getty Images pp. 18 (Popperfoto/ Captain Robert Falcon Scott), 31 (The Image Bank/Ken Graham); NASA pp. 10, 13; Naturepl.com p.8 (Ben Osborne); NOC Southampton pp. 24 (Andy Webb), 29 (Katy Sheen), San Diego Supercomputer Center, UC San Diego p. 16 (Matt Mazloff); Science Photo Library p. 17 (Dee Breger), Shutterstock pp. 42 boots (Aptyp_koK), 42 coffee (magicoven), 42 cookie (Sergio33), 42 hand (DenisNata), 42 wind vane (Gwoeii); SuperStock p. 9 (Juice Images). Design elements Shutterstock.

Cover photo of the *James Clark Ross* reproduced with permission of BAS/Pete Bucktrout.

Every effort has been made to contact copyright holders of material reproduced in this book. Any omissions will be rectified in subsequent printings if notice is given to the publisher.

All the internet addresses (URLs) given in this book were valid at the time of going to press. However, due to the dynamic nature of the internet, some addresses may have changed, or sites may have changed or ceased to exist since publication. While the author and publisher regret any inconvenience this may cause readers, no responsibility for any such changes can be accepted by either the author or the publisher.

contents

I'm Emily Shuckburgh, Head of the Open Oceans research group at the British Antarctic Survey (BAS). It's chilly here on Antarctica's Southern Ocean, but the science is exciting!

My amazing magic moment happened back in the year 2000. It was my first time as a member of a science team in the Arctic.

We were releasing science research balloons into the atmosphere. As the balloons rose, they dazzled in the sunlight, and the wispy clouds around them shimmered with all the colours of the rainbow above the snowy landscape. It was spectacular.

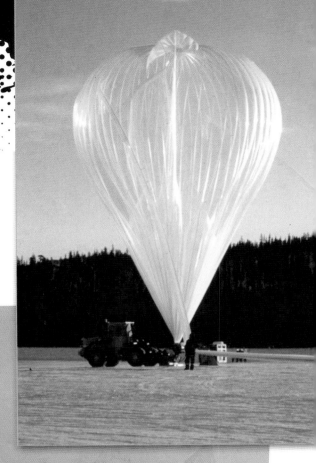

We sent the balloons up to investigate the destruction of the ozone layer, which creates an invisible filter that acts like a protective sunscreen around Earth. It shields Earth from the Sun's harmful ultraviolet (UV) rays that can burn our skin. In recent decades, the layer has thinned.

Did you know?

The clouds I saw were made of frozen crystals, which only form in polar winter temperatures of below −78 degrees Celsius (−108 degrees Fahrenheit). Sunlight shining through the crystals makes rainbow colours. Chemical changes occur on the surface of these crystals, releasing chlorine from the gases (CFCs) once used in aerosol cans and refrigerators. In springtime, the stronger sunlight acts on the chlorine in the atmosphere, destroying the protective ozone layer around Earth.

NOTE TO SELF

The work I do tries to shed light on environmental change and its effects on the planet. This science needs a lot of maths and I'm a trained mathematician. Could there be any better way of using my skills?

THE IMPORTANCE OF ANTARCTICA

My research is on climate change and focuses on Antarctica's Southern Ocean and the atmosphere above it. We are trying to find out how climate change affects Antarctica and how changes there affect the rest of the planet. This ocean is a special place to research because it actually helps the world to slow climate change. We need this help because Earth's climate is getting warmer.

We monitor the atmosphere, ocean, sea ice and ice sheets for changes.

Normally, the Sun warms Earth, and carbon gases form a blanket that traps heat around our planet. This is called the natural greenhouse effect. But humans burn a lot of fossil fuels, such as coal, oil and gas, releasing extra carbon gases into the atmosphere. These form a thicker blanket that traps more heat around Earth, causing our climate to change.

The Southern Ocean helps us by soaking up about 10 per cent of the carbon dioxide humans put into the atmosphere each year. This slows climate change. But how long can the ocean keep absorbing carbon? Finding answers is my voyage of discovery.

In March 2008, the W
Shelf on the rapidly wa
Antarctic Peninsula su
collapsed. It lost more
square kilometres (160
miles) of its ice.

20 metres

Did you know?

Antarctica's ice sheet is the largest ice mass on Earth. In summer, there is less ice and it still covers almost 14 million square kilometres (5.4 million square miles). This ice reflects about 80 per cent of the Sun's rays, helping to keep Earth cool.

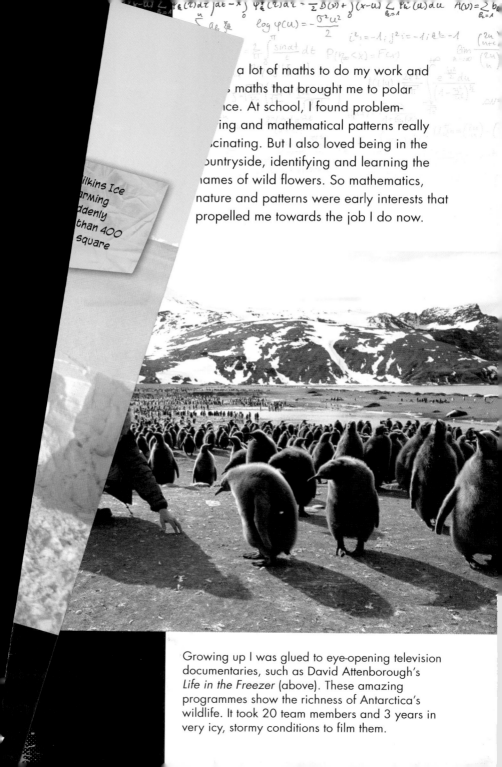

a lot of maths to do my work and maths that brought me to polar ice. At school, I found problem-ing and mathematical patterns really cinating. But I also loved being in the untryside, identifying and learning the ames of wild flowers. So mathematics, nature and patterns were early interests that propelled me towards the job I do now.

Growing up I was glued to eye-opening television documentaries, such as David Attenborough's *Life in the Freezer* (above). These amazing programmes show the richness of Antarctica's wildlife. It took 20 team members and 3 years in very icy, stormy conditions to film them.

Children still enjoy practical science and maths at the Royal Institution, the oldest independent science research body in the world.

In the 1980s, I also tuned in to a weekly British science and technology television series called *Tomorrow's World*. Programmes like this showed an increasing amount of research on the growth of ozone holes and environmental change. I was inspired to become a scientist myself!

MY HERO!
Judith Hann
(born 1942)

Judith presented *Tomorrow's World* between 1974 and 1994. Judith is a zoologist – an animal expert – but is passionate about many fields of science and the environment.

NOTE TO SELF

I often think of the great time I had at Saturday Mathematics Masterclasses held by the Royal Institution. The classes showed maths in the real world. At last I had proper problems to solve. I saw the possibilities of maths – and the fun!

I went on to study maths at university. Afterwards, I began to use my maths in weather forecasting and climate change. It helped me to set up my own weather company. I wanted to help people plan their businesses and lives.

Maths can explain the swirling cloud patterns seen in this satellite image. Here, they have been formed as the wind has hit Jan Mayen Island in the Greenland Sea.

WEATHER AND CLIMATE

Weather is what we experience over a short period such as a week, while climate occurs over a long period, such as 30 years. I use maths to forecast tomorrow's weather by putting today's weather data, including temperature and air pressure, into a computer simulation. It can be quite difficult to predict weather, because even slight changes in data can make a massive difference to the forecast.

A scientist launches a weather balloon. This carries a small package of instruments that measure temperature, pressure and humidity up to a height of 25 kilometres (15 miles). Launches occur every day throughout the year.

Did you know?

Scientists study how tiny changes at the beginning of a system, such as the weather, can have a big impact. We call this impact chaos theory. It also teaches us that nature works in patterns, and patterns are what my work is all about.

I use a similar computer simulation to predict the climate, but I need to input data on the amount of carbon dioxide in the atmosphere. I am particularly interested in the patterns of winds and ocean currents and how they change over time. Swirling patterns known as eddies form storm systems in the atmosphere and are also found in the ocean.

TOOLS OF THE TRADE: WEATHER BALLOONS

Weather balloons carry bundles of instruments called radiosondes, which contain sensors that measure temperature, atmospheric pressure, wind and humidity. Instruments called transponders send the data back to computers on Earth. High-rising weather balloons won't pop easily, as they're made of a material that can resist pressure way up in the atmosphere.

BOUND FOR THE POLES

After a higher degree called a doctorate, I continued studies that led me in 2000 to the Arctic and my magic moment (see pages 4–5). The use of CFCs that thin the ozone layer had been banned in 1989, in an international treaty called the Montreal Protocol. But old CFCs are still very active in the atmosphere.

Did you know?

The Arctic and the Antarctic are both frozen worlds, but in many ways they are poles apart! The North Pole is in the Arctic and the South Pole is in the Antarctic. The Arctic is an ocean surrounded by an icy continent, but the Antarctic is an icy continent surrounded by ocean. The Arctic tern travels each year from its Arctic breeding grounds to its wintering grounds off Antarctica, covering some 40,000 kilometres (25,000 miles)! This is the farthest yearly journey of any bird.

MY HERO!
Joseph Farman
(1930–2013)

On my first field trip, I met the incredible Professor Joseph Farman. Every year since 1956, he'd measured ozone levels in the atmosphere above Antarctica. In 1985, Joe alerted a disbelieving world to the ozone "holes".

MY HERO!

Susan Solomon
(born 1956)

I was inspired to study polar science by Susan Solomon. She is an expert on the chemistry of the ozone hole and on climate change and has led science expeditions to Antarctica. She has also written a great book about the weather conditions on Captain Scott's fatal South Pole expedition.

ozone hole

This NASA satellite image over Antarctica's ozone hole was taken in 2012, during September, a month when ozone is thin. It is shown by the blue and purple colours.

MEASURING OZONE LEVELS

MEASURING OZONE LEVELS

MEASURING OZONE LEVELS

MEASURING OZONE LEVELS

I learnt a lot from the way Joe Farman (see page 12) did his science. Joe had measured ozone levels in Antarctica every year with old Dobson spectrometers, instruments invented in 1924. He was passionate about patient, hands-on data collecting. In my own science, I often use computer models, but I also test them with real experiments in Antarctica's icy waters.

Joe (left) and his team were so astounded by the low ozone readings that they ordered new Dobson spectrometers to double-check them. They recorded even lower levels!

Polar bears now find it difficult to feed in summer on ice floes in some parts of Hudson Bay because many have melted. Their habitat is being altered by climate change.

I like to keep in touch with how climate change affects people and the environment. So on my first field trips to Canada's Arctic region, I got talking to some locals. They told me that in the past, at Christmas time, they sledged across the ice on Hudson Bay from their village to the main town, Iqaluit. But for many years now the ice has been too thin. Is this due to climate change? It's my job to find out.

TOOLS OF THE TRADE: SATELLITE IMAGES

We use satellite images and data to measure ice and snow melt. The Arctic Sea ice melts over the summer, reaching its minimum extent in September each year. But this is now just half what it was 30 years ago.

ANSWERS IN THE POLAR OCEAN

I was now sure that I wanted to find some answers to climate change in the motion of the Southern Ocean and the atmosphere above it. So I took up research posts, working with great scientists in France and the United States.

In 2009, I became Head of Open Oceans for the British Antarctic Survey. So my working life is now dedicated to the Poles. There, I focus on the circulation and global influence of the Arctic Ocean, and the Southern Ocean around Antarctica.

This is Antarctic Circumpolar Current (ACC) in the Southern Ocean. Slow-moving currents are shown in blue and fast-moving currents in red. The volume of its waters is the same as 500 Amazon Rivers! Any change occurring in the ACC affects the Atlantic, Pacific and Indian Ocean systems connected to it.

We're especially interested in eddies, which are like atmospheric storms, but in the oceans. These pools of swirling, churning waters, blown by fierce winds, can change the oceans' circulation. This can affect the way old carbon layers from the seabed are churned up and how much carbon the ocean absorbs from the atmosphere.

Satellite images capture huge swirling areas of tiny sea plants called phytoplankton, which show how a current is moving. They absorb carbon dioxide, which they need to grow. So they are a good indicator of carbon levels in the sea.

Did you know?

The world's coal, oil and gas reserves contain about 500 billion tonnes of carbon, which can be released into the atmosphere when we burn it for fuel. But there are a massive 6,000 billion tonnes of it lying at the bottom of our oceans in marine sediments.

Preparing for Antarctica

Field trips to the Arctic prepared me a little for my first expedition to Antarctica. But only a little! For Antarctica is the chilliest, windiest continent on Earth. In winter, temperatures can drop to −60 degrees Celsius (−78 degrees Fahrenheit). Howling winds can speed along at over 160 kilometres (100 miles) per hour. And with whipped-up snow and ice, it can be really hard to see. The summer months, when I go, are a bit warmer, although the wind can still blow hard.

MY HERO!

Captain Robert Falcon Scott (1868–1912)

Captain Robert Falcon Scott is most famous for his heroic 1912 expedition to the South Pole, where he died with his team (above) on the Ross Ice Shelf. But I admire him also for his serious scientific aims, choosing a team that gave us so much knowledge on Antarctica's climate, geology, flora, fauna, magnetism and fossils.

On our Polar science vessel in the Southern Ocean, even faster winds can churn up colossal 12-metre (40-foot) waves, even in summer. We can't do science when conditions are like this. Even when it's calmer, we find the icy cold difficult to cope with sometimes. And seasickness can be a problem for some of the team.

Did you know?

Most of my field science takes place in summer because the seas freeze over in winter. But marine biologists go in winter to study life under the ice. They also observe the effects of global temperature changes on the lives of Antarctica's amazing creatures, such as the Emperor penguin.

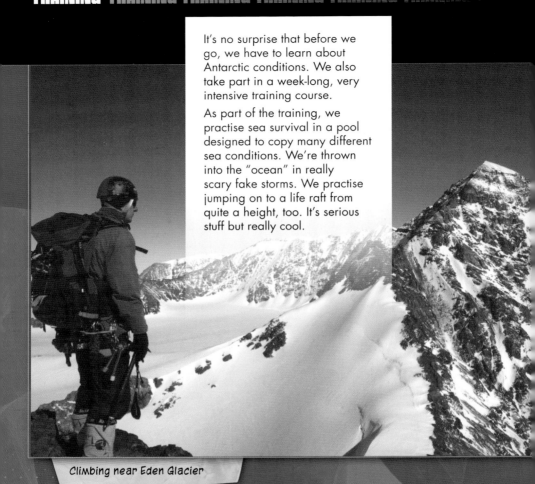

It's no surprise that before we go, we have to learn about Antarctic conditions. We also take part in a week-long, very intensive training course.

As part of the training, we practise sea survival in a pool designed to copy many different sea conditions. We're thrown into the "ocean" in really scary fake storms. We practise jumping on to a life raft from quite a height, too. It's serious stuff but really cool.

Climbing near Eden Glacier

TOOLS OF THE TRADE: TOOLS FOR CLIMBING MOUNTAINS

Some science takes place up Antarctica's icy mountains. To climb them we need ice axes, ice screws and crampons over our boots to help grip the ice. The brittle ice is formed from snow that compacted over countless years. Newer snow is fragile, so snow anchors are needed. These are metal bars buried deep, with ropes attached to them.

This is Drake Passage, where I work on the Southern Ocean. When this picture was taken, there was a Force 12 gale, and I couldn't do my experiments in that!

NOTE TO SELF

First Aid skills are hugely important. We're trained to cope with human casualties by practising on professional actors. They're scarily good at pretending to roll around in pain with severe injuries. There's a lot of fake blood, too!

WELL DRESSED AND WELL FED

Our bodies can never adjust to extreme cold, so we learn how to dress for it. Light layers are best as they trap air, which is warmed by our body's heat. The first is the "wicking layer". This draws sweat away from the skin into outer layers, where it evaporates. It's really important to keep dry.

I'M wearing a hat because you lose 20 per cent of body heat from your head! Wrists, ankles and neck are also heat-loss hot spots.

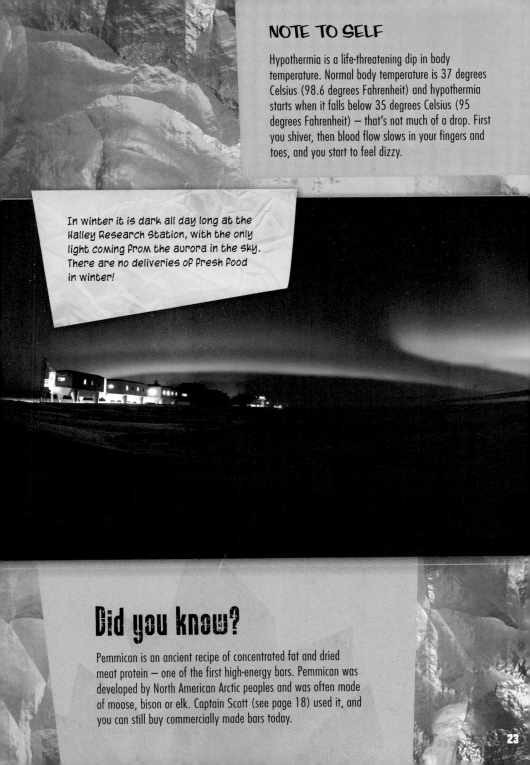

NOTE TO SELF

Hypothermia is a life-threatening dip in body temperature. Normal body temperature is 37 degrees Celsius (98.6 degrees Fahrenheit) and hypothermia starts when it falls below 35 degrees Celsius (95 degrees Fahrenheit) — that's not much of a drop. First you shiver, then blood flow slows in your fingers and toes, and you start to feel dizzy.

In winter it is dark all day long at the Halley Research Station, with the only light coming from the aurora in the sky. There are no deliveries of fresh food in winter!

Did you know?

Pemmican is an ancient recipe of concentrated fat and dried meat protein — one of the first high-energy bars. Pemmican was developed by North American Arctic peoples and was often made of moose, bison or elk. Captain Scott (see page 18) used it, and you can still buy commercially made bars today.

THE RRS *JAMES CLARK ROSS*

So now I'm ready to join the RRS *James Clark Ross*, the science ship that will be my home and my workplace for many weeks to come. Welcome aboard! The *James Clark Ross* is a floating laboratory where scientists examine seawater and biological specimens. It's where a whole host of data about the ocean is collected.

The *James Clark Ross* has many special features to cope with icy conditions and to assist scientific experiments. The ship can be steered very slowly through flat sea ice that is a metre (3.3 feet) thick and rolls slightly so that the ice does not squeeze the hull.

It has been designed to move quietly so that underwater acoustic equipment can deliver accurate results.

This is an Autonomous Underwater Vehicle. We can now send ones like this beneath the ice to take measurements of the ocean underneath.

While the waters of the Southern Ocean are my main focus, there are many other projects that we can do from the ship. One of these is measuring the thickness of the ice over a period of time. This can tell us how much heat is lost from the ocean to the atmosphere – a process that affects climate.

TOOLS OF THE TRADE: ICE MASS BALANCE BUOYS

You can see from the picture that the RRS *James Clark Ross* is offloading ice mass balance buoys to measure ice thickness. Among other instruments, these buoys carry digital chips that record temperature, and some even have webcams.

SECRETS IN THE SEA

We take water samples in the Southern Ocean to see its temperature and how salty it is. This can tell us where the water has come from. We can detect surprisingly warm, salty water that came from the North Atlantic and travelled south in the ocean circulation. Our measurements look for changes over time in this circulation. We also take measurements to help us understand how the Southern Ocean influences the climate across Earth.

But it's not just our climate that depends on the chilly waters around Antarctica. Amazingly, the Southern Ocean supplies nutrients that fertilize 75 per cent of plant and animal growth in the rest of the world's oceans!

NOTE TO SELF

One of the great things about working in Antarctica is that I know there are teams from 30 nations here. There's often cooperation between us, for example the British Antarctic Survey and the US National Science Foundation worked together on a high altitude balloon campaign to collect data from the atmosphere.

Here we are lowering a circular frame into the water with 24 Niskin bottles that we can open and close at different depths to take water samples.

Here we are emptying the Niskin bottles to analyse the water in the laboratory on the ship. We measure the amount of salt and other chemicals.

MY HERO!

Captain Robert Fitzroy
(1805–1865)

Captain Robert Fitzroy sailed the *Beagle* to the edge of the Southern Ocean with the famous scientist Charles Darwin on board. Using navigation charts, thermometers, barometers and excellent record keeping, Fitzroy became the world's first weather forecaster and made meteorology a proper science. In 1854, he established the UK's National Weather Service, which is now known as the Met Office.

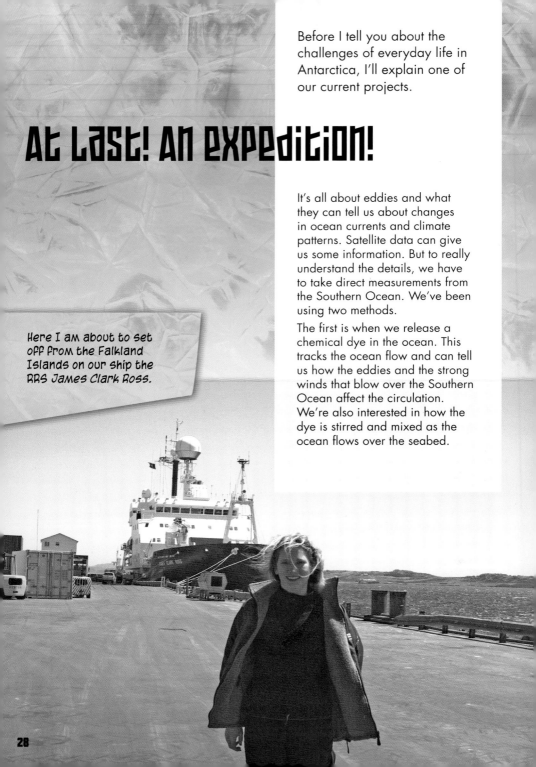

Before I tell you about the challenges of everyday life in Antarctica, I'll explain one of our current projects.

At Last! An Expedition!

It's all about eddies and what they can tell us about changes in ocean currents and climate patterns. Satellite data can give us some information. But to really understand the details, we have to take direct measurements from the Southern Ocean. We've been using two methods.

The first is when we release a chemical dye in the ocean. This tracks the ocean flow and can tell us how the eddies and the strong winds that blow over the Southern Ocean affect the circulation. We're also interested in how the dye is stirred and mixed as the ocean flows over the seabed.

Here I am about to set off from the Falkland Islands on our ship the RRS James Clark Ross.

I'm most interested in the second method of taking measurements from the Southern Ocean. To do this, we drop floats down into the water and follow their course as they bob around like rubber ducks in the ocean currents. We use these floats to trace out the patterns of mixing created by the eddies.

This equipment detects the concentration of dye in seawater.

TOOLS OF THE TRADE: ROBOTIC FLOATS

There are more than 3,000 robotic floats in the world's oceans! Some drift at the sea surface, while others are deep-diving, taking measurements of temperature and saltiness. These transmit their data back via satellites when they reach the surface. Some are tracked acoustically while they're under water. That means they're traced by using equipment that bounces sound off them.

USING ECHOSOUNDERS

So now we're on the Southern Ocean, buffeted by wind and waves. Here, the Circumpolar Current rushes through the narrow point at Drake Passage between Antarctica and South America, swirling with eddies as it goes.

Unlocking the secrets of our oceans' currents involves other areas of research, such as measuring the seabed's hills and valleys over which the sea passes. A huge instrument called an echosounder collects the measurements. The data is then used to create maps.

TOOLS OF THE TRADE: ECHOSOUNDER

From the ship's hull, an echosounder sends out beams of sound that hit the seabed, then return to a transducer, which measures the journey time for each hit. A short journey time, for example, means that the seabed at that point rises close to the surface.

ship
(front view)

ship
(side view)

transducer

transducer

transmitted and returned
sound pulses

transmitted and returned
sound pulses

seabed

seabed

We also need to know the chemical make-up of Antarctica's seawater. In our on-board laboratories, the sea's acidity is measured. This is because when the ocean absorbs more carbon, it becomes more acidic. In January 2013, the BAS led a team of 30 scientists to test for acidity and its effects on marine life, such as dissolving sea-snail shells.

Did you know?

International treaties are for the moment protecting Antarctica from oil exploration and mining, unlike in the Arctic. Climate change is melting the sea ice in the Arctic, opening it up to transit by ships and allowing oil and mining companies to tap into previously untapped reserves.

The Arctic holds about 30 per cent of the planet's untapped natural gas reserves and 13 per cent of its oil.

A day in the Life

It's another thrilling day on the RRS *James Clark Ross*. Will the weather allow us to deliver our packed science schedule? I can relax a little, knowing that I'm part of a great team of scientists. Our expeditions usually last at least six weeks, so teamwork is essential.

Here I am with my team from the night shift!

My "working day" is often my "working night"! We operate 24-hour days, so the ship and the science never sleep. Each of us sticks to the same shift on an expedition. So it could be from 8.00 a.m. to 4.00 p.m.; from 4.00 p.m. to midnight; or from midnight to 8.00 a.m. Sometimes these 8-hour shifts extend to 12 hours so we can complete the day's work.

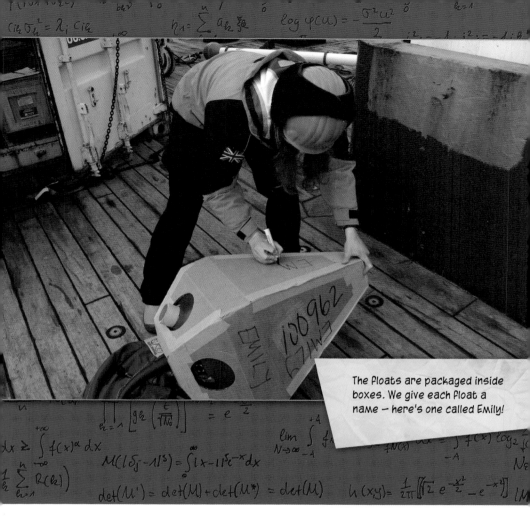

The floats are packaged inside boxes. We give each float a name — here's one called Emily!

$\left[g_k \left(\dfrac{\epsilon}{TN_0} \right) \right] = e^{-\frac{u}{2}}$

$dx \geq \int_{-\infty}^{+\infty} f(x)^a \, dx \qquad M(|\delta_j - \mathbb{1}|^s) = \int_0^\infty |x-1|^s \bar{e}^{-x} dx \qquad \lim_{N \to \infty} \int_{-A}^{+A} f \qquad \int_{-A}^{+A} f(x) \log_2 f$

$\tfrac{1}{k} \sum_{i=1}^{n} R(k_i) \qquad \det(M') = \det(M) + \det(M^*) = \det(M) \qquad h(xy) = \dfrac{1}{2\pi} \left[\sqrt{2} \, e^{-\frac{x^2}{2}} - e^{-x^2} \right]$

I GOT THE NIGHT SHIFT!

So it's 8.00 a.m. I've just finished the night shift, but there's a team meeting before I can eat and get some rest. Our chief scientist sets the goals and the ship's captain tells us if it's safe to go ahead with them.

TOOLS OF THE TRADE: DROGUED FLOATS

Last night we were setting floats into the water at points where satellite information pointed to eddies. The floats are spherical, with a drogue parachute attached to each. This parachute stabilizes the float and makes sure that ocean currents, not the wind, are moving it.

After the meeting I tuck into my dinner – the chefs cook some great meals! I go to bed, but the rolling waves make sleep difficult.

After an early evening "breakfast", I write up notes on our experiments, and then go on deck for the day's task. This time we're pulling in devices called a CDT (Conductivity, Depth and Temperature) and a VMP (Vertical Microstructure Profiler). CDTs take vital measurements of chemicals in the ocean. VMPs help tell us where the ocean's mixing occurs.

But the VMP has got lost! The wind's whipping up the waves and we're blowing off course, so locating it is not an easy task. It's summertime in Antarctica, so daylight lasts almost all night long. It's hard to spot the light on the VMP, but finally its flag is sighted!

Flocks of birds help us locate our VMPs! And shoals of fish, whales and dolphins also seem to be really curious about our instruments!

VMP

After a quick lunch, the crew uses winches to haul up the CDT frame. We remove the bottles and take them to the on-board laboratory for analysis.

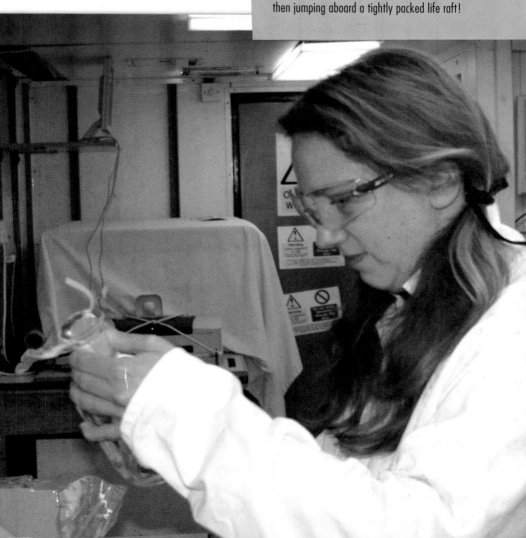

I'm testing samples for carbon gases using a dangerous chemical called mercuric chloride. So I have to wear a science gown and protective goggles.

science on ice

research stations on land. Or I should say, on ice! Because about 96 per cent of Antarctica is covered with snow and ice all year round.

Sometimes I visit our research stations on land. Or I should say, on ice! Because about 96 per cent of Antarctica is covered with snow and ice all year round.

The tiny four per cent left is mainly bare rock with a little vegetation – some mosses, lichens, a little grass and just two species of flower. However, this area of vegetation is larger than it was, which is possibly another sign of climate change.

Did you know?

We're trying hard to develop environmentally friendly technology to run our stations. Our waste is shipped well away from Antarctica for disposal. On one trip, our ship stopped at Damoy Point to dig out and remove two old broken snowmobiles. We all have to muck in!

This is Rothera Research Station built on the Antarctic Peninsula's Adelaide Island.

My work takes me to Rothera Research Station, which is a large complex that includes science laboratories, offices, workshops, a hangar for aircraft, a landing stage for ships and an operations control tower. We even get to relax in a recreation area. Things have moved on since Joe Farman's day. He had to melt snow just to make a cup of tea!

NOTE TO SELF

I like linking up with other scientists, whose work adds to the big picture. For example, we can now track how species adapted to climate change in the past through

Getting around on a snowmobile is fun! It also allows me to see field science research, such as ice-core sampling. In recent years, ice cores have given us an amazing window into climate change going back 800,000 years. Ice cores show us that current carbon gas levels are higher than at any other time since then. For my projects, they reveal previous cycles of ice age freezing and melting, and how the amount of carbon stored in the Southern Ocean changes as the temperature changes.

Above, some scientists drill down and get samples of ice core. As layer after layer of snow builds up, tiny bubbles of air are trapped in the ice. You can see those bubbles in this slice of ice core (right).

NOTE TO SELF

Antarctica holds so many surprises, such as carbon gas bubbles that pop from melting ice cores. If I get close enough to the bubbles, I can breathe in air that's hundreds of thousands of years old. This is from a time when the earliest forms of humankind had only just started gathering around campfires. Amazing!

We couldn't do without our light aircraft. As well as mapping Antarctica and other activities, they also take us home. Our Twin Otter aircraft take off on skis rather than wheels along an icy glacier strip (see below).

Did you know?

Antarctica has ice that is up to 4.7 kilometres (2.9 miles) thick. This ice preserves a record of climate conditions exactly at the time it was frozen. It gives us the amounts of gases in the atmosphere and the temperature at that time.

Looking ahead

I hope you can now see that the Poles are really special places, where stunning scenery and wildlife are matched by amazing scientific phenomena on both sea and land. They are places where nature gives us so many clues to climate change. We just have to work hard at finding the answers.

NOTE TO SELF

By the way, I never forgot who inspired me to follow my dreams as a mathematician and scientist. In 1999, I joined the *Tomorrow's World* team (see page 9), hopefully encouraging young mathematicians to become polar scientists, too.

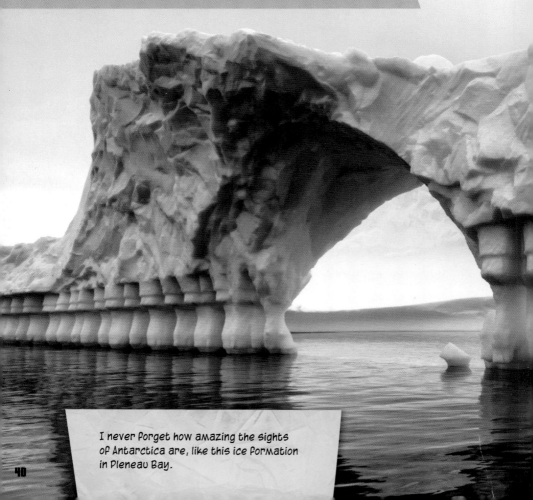

I never forget how amazing the sights of Antarctica are, like this ice formation in Pleneau Bay.

I'm passionate about communicating our scientific discoveries to many different groups, from politicians to leaders of industry. Studying the atmosphere, oceans and ice at the Poles has helped us conclude that humans are disrupting the climate by putting carbon dioxide into the atmosphere.

Unless we find alternatives, the climate will be disrupted further, with substantial changes not just at the Poles but across the world. Will human creativity solve this problem? It is up to each and every one of us to do our bit!

Did you know?

In 2013, top scientists from around the world confirmed human-made climate change in a report by the Intergovernmental Panel on Climate Change (IPCC). The report makes some environmental predictions for the future. One of these is that sea levels could rise by about 0.5–1 metres (about 1.5–3 feet) by the end of the century if we continue to put carbon dioxide into the atmosphere as now.

QUIZ

Have you got what it takes to become a polar scientist?

1. It's winter and there's snow on the ground. Do you...

a) Stay indoors, shivering in front of the radiator?

b) Run straight outside and play in the freezing cold?

c) Put on warm clothes, boots and a hat, then go outside?

2. You are taken to a science and technology museum. Which of these do you do?

a) Look quickly at the exhibits and then find the café.

b) Head straight for the café and stay there.

c) Look carefully at all the exhibits and take part in the interactive ones.

3. You make a weather vane at school. You are then asked to take it home and record the direction of the wind every day on your two-week holiday. Do you...

a) Take measurements, but only for the first week?

b) Forget to set up the weather vane?

c) Take measurements every day and create a chart showing the results?

If you answered mostly Cs, you should think about becoming a polar scientist!

42

How much can you remember about what you've read in this book?

1. Which type of gases destroy ozone in the atmosphere?

2. What type of gas increases climate change?

3. How fast can the wind blow in Antarctica?

4. True or false? Humans put carbon dioxide into the atmosphere by burning fossil fuels such as gas, coal and oil.

5. Unscramble these letters to spell the name of an instrument that measures the thickness of the ozone layer from the ground. Hint: There are two words.

    ctseordeompbnosret

6. True or false? The thinning of the ozone layer is the major cause of global warming.

7. How thick can the ice in Antarctica measure at its deepest point?

ANSWERS

1. CFCs
2. Carbon dioxide
3. Winds can blow over 160 kilometres (100 miles) per hour.
4. True
5. Dobson spectrometer
6. False
7. 4.7 kilometres (2.9 miles)

43

Glossary

air pressure force of air above us down on Earth. Air pressure measurements help predict weather.

atmosphere layers of gases high above Earth

carbon dioxide one of the carbon gases that are also called greenhouse gases

chaos theory idea that tiny changes within a system can have a big impact on the system as a whole, such as the weather system

CFC chlorofluorocarbon gas that destroys the protective ozone layer in the atmosphere around Earth

climate typical weather that occurs over a long period of time

computer simulation computer program that represents something in the real world

crampon spiky metal frame around a climbing shoe to help climbers grip ice

drogue parachute parachute attached to a science float. It makes sure that ocean currents are moving the float, not the wind.

eddy like a storm in the atmosphere, but occurring in the oceans

fauna animal life

flora plant life

geology study of Earth's rock structure

hypothermia when the body becomes dangerously cold and starts to shut down

ice core very long tube of ice dug out of huge ice sheets. Ice cores tell us a lot about past climate change.

lichen small plant-like organism. It is a mixture of plant parts and fungus parts.

magnetism force between objects producing areas around them that attract or push away other objects. Magnetism is strongest at the Poles.

meteorology study of the processes and behaviour of the atmosphere, usually to forecast the weather

nutrient food

ozone invisible layer of gases that surround Earth, protecting it from the Sun, a bit like a sunscreen

pemmican food with high fat and dried protein in it. It is eaten in cold climates to provide energy.

phytoplankton tiny sea plants that start Earth's food chain

radiosonde bundle of instruments that measure weather data in the atmosphere. They are attached to high-rising weather balloons.

sediment rocks and soils washed down from the land to the seabed or riverbed

snow anchor strong metal bar buried deep in snow with a rope attached to help climbers in snowy conditions

snowmobile open motorized vehicle designed to ride over snow and ice

ultraviolet (UV) invisible wavelengths of light that come from the Sun. Too many UV rays reaching Earth can burn people's skin.

weather conditions such as temperature, wind, sunshine and rain

Find Out More

BOOKS

100 Facts: Polar Lands, Steve Parker
(Miles Kelly Publishing, 2010)

Climate Change (Eco Alert), Rebecca Hunter
(Franklin Watts, 2012)

Climate Change (Eyewitness), John Woodward
(Dorling Kindersley, 2011)

Climate Change (Headline Issues), Angela Royston
(Heinemann Library, 2010)

How to Survive in Antarctica, Lucy Jane Bledsoe (Holiday House,
2006)

Polar Survival Handbook (Explore Your World), Jen Green
(Miles Kelly Publishing, 2012)

WEBSITES

http://discoveringantarctica.org.uk
This excellent website features activities and fact sheets.

www.antarctica.ac.uk/staff-profiles/webspace/emsh/bio.html
For more on Emily's work and studies, see her British Antarctic
Survey web page.

www.antarctica.ac.uk/images/video/player.php?id=012d8f70
For a spectacular view of the collapsing Wilkins Ice Shelf, see
this video shot from an aeroplane.